A Motivational Journey

Tiffany N. McMorris

i

ACKNOWLEDGEMENTS

I want to first give thanks to the lord above. Thank you for every obstacle I've encountered in life, whether it was failing or excelling. Had it not been for my trials, I would have never experienced my triumphs.

To my mother, God rest her soul, I wish you were here, so that I could personally tell you, from the NEW ME, THANK YOU MOM! I love you and will miss you forever. I am so blessed that God chose you for me.

To MY BABIES, mom loves you more than life. You all are the reason why I go so hard. Destiny, Jasmyne and Dennis, thank you for molding me into the mother I am today, each one of you play a major part in my motivational journey. I pray that I inspire you to be whatever you desire to be in life. Remember, anything that you put your mind to can be done.

To Dennis, the love of my life, thank you for loving me and listening to all my out of the box, Gemini thoughts. I appreciate you for never telling me that things couldn't be done, and always helping me to believe that they could. Thank you for supporting me in anything I want to do, I will forever love you.

To my publisher, you are a pure gem and I am forever grateful for you. Thank you for your constant push for me to just start and putting up with all my stuff. I love you beyond words and I appreciate you beyond this side of life Suga.

XOXO- Tfne Ncole

DEDICATION

To my mother Tonya L. McMorris,

Your profound determination for me to reach a level a maturity has manifested!

Thank you for loving me unconditionally and giving me spiritual wisdom.

INTRODUCTION

Have you ever been exhausted with thinking about how you would find the motivation within yourself, to accomplish your goals, or just to complete simple tasks?

Better yet, have you asked yourself, "what really motivates me?"

Do you find yourself questioning why you aren't motivated?

Have you ever connected with another individuals, exchanging mind blowing ideas, only to realize that neither of you can motivate the other?
 One thing you must realize is that you must look within to discover what truly motivates

you. Only then can you seek support from others to stay motivated.

A *Motivational Journey* will help you discover your intrinsic motivators. This journal will also help you to find ways to stay motivated, believe in and encourage yourself.

I'm a firm believer that you must always channel your energy. For example, find your inner strength and cultivate your circle, enriching it with more goal driven people. Removing negative influences and changing the tone of your thoughts. By doing so, you align yourself in the right place where great energy will coincide. There are some instances that you may initially perceive as negative, but I once read a book called *The 5 Second Rule: Transform your Life, Work, and Confidence* with *Everyday Courage* by Mel Robbins. This book taught me how to overcome this. *The 5 Second Rule* is a must read! If you apply the rule when negativity strikes, you will do amazing at staying positive and motivated!

In this book, I can only give you the tools I used along my journey of motivation. I was motivated to become a better and more positive person overall. Once I began motivating myself and speaking motivating words over my life, my thought process changed tremendously. The way I viewed things started to change and I stopped seeing everything from a negative perspective. In completing this journal, my heart is for you to experience growth, peace and of course motivation to accomplish and overcome anything your heart desire.

Rule #1

You must first Trust God. Allow His voice to enter your spirit, so that you understand the path He desires for you to take. He is talking just be still, listen and reflect!

Speak positive words into your atmosphere. Once you make speaking positivity over your life a habit, you will start to see your journey in a positive way.

I've prepared 30 days of motivating quotes along with scripture references, to help direct your path toward finding and keeping your motivation, as well as encourage yourself.

I hope to inspire you and I ask that you allow God into your heart, just as I did!

Remember, this is your journey and yours alone. Don't be too hard on yourself, stay motivated, and be excited to celebrate YOU along the way!

-TfneNcole

YOUR JOURNEY

<u>Day 1</u>

There's beauty in each journey, even if you have yet to discover it, it is there. You may not know exactly how you will discover beauty in your journey but be intentional in finding and appreciating it.

Trust the process!

Stay Motivated!

Genesis 24:42 NIV
When I came to the spring today, I said, 'LORD, God of my master Abraham, if you will, please grant success to the journey on which I have come.

What journey are you on, that requires your motivation?

_____

_____

_____

_____

_____

_____

_____

_____

_____

_____

_____

_____

_____

YOUR WHY

Day 2

Remember why you started? Never forget why you were motivated to accomplish the goals you set for your life. Stand in your truth.

It is funny how life goes. Just when you are well on your way to entering a new level of growth, here comes adversity.

Do not give up! It is YOUR DREAM, and it has been a passion that has been within you for so long, you just have not had the drive or in other words motivation to get to the finish line.

What is your dream? Why do you desire to accomplish it?

FAITH

Day 3

Try Faith!
Everyday 24:7 -TfneNcole

Now faith is confidence in what we hope for and assurance about what we do not see. Hebrews 11:1NIV

When you have faith every day, you will begin to see dramatic results within. Take this time to think about where your faith is.

What does faith mean for you?

How is your faith today?

GUIDE

Day 4

God will guide you to and through the best path for your life.

But will you follow him, as he advises and guides! - TfneNcole

How will you follow God's path?

_____

_____

_____

_____

_____

_____

_____

_____

_____

_____

_____

_____

_____

COMFORT ZONE

Day 5

If what you are doing is familiar, you haven't stepped outside of your comfort zone! -TfneNcole

What comfort zone roadblocks are hindering you from accomplishing your goals.

_____

_____

_____

_____

_____

_____

_____

_____

_____

_____

_____

_____

_____

FOCUS

Day 6

Dear God,
If you see me starting to give up, please
keep me going! -TfneNcole

Take a few minutes to reflect on any areas in your life that require more focus. Write them down and work on them daily.

*Be You and only you!
The only person you
should want to be better
than, is the person you
were yesterday!
-TfneNcole*

Day 7

We are always looking to compare ourselves and take note on how the next person is doing. Think about the time we spend looking at what others are doing. That time could be spent on doing the work to become a better you.

Never compare yourself to anyone. Always motivate yourself to be better than you think you can be! Because you CAN!

*It is okay to be different,
stay outside the box,
because you will never fit
in it!*
-TfneNcole

Day 8

Think about a box and how tight it can get if you climb into it.

People who choose to stay in the proverbial box, are too busy being like each other, while you are on the outside making better opportunities for yourself!

If you stay outside the box; chances are, you will most likely come out better than people who chose to stay inside the box.

PASS OUT LOVE DAILY!
-TfneNcole

Day 9

Love is an unconditional affection with no limits or conditions.

Love is a great interest and pleasure in something. Our greatest interest should be ourselves!

Learning how to love ourselves properly, increases our ability to properly love others.

Whether it is the lady at the grocery store or a random stranger who may need encouragement, pass out love.

Spreading love freely can help any individual however, it must first start with you.

ENCOURAGE YOURSELF!

Day 10

Encouragement works like an energy pills, that can give us the strength that we need to overcome the obstacles between us, and our goals.

Write down 5 encouraging words and
sentences to say to yourself daily.

_____

_____

_____

_____

_____

_____

_____

_____

_____

_____

_____

_____

_____

_____

AMBITION

Day 11

Having ambition means that you want to achieve certain things in life. Being ambitious will expose you to things unseen.

Stay ambitious to get across the finish line!

How can you be more ambitious?

_____

_____

_____

_____

_____

_____

_____

_____

_____

_____

_____

_____

ENERGY

Day 12

This word has never meant as much to me as it does now that I have reached a different level of growth.

Protecting your energy is required to reach the next level of growth. Think about it, if you never protect what is ultimately needed lo succeed how do you think you will advance?

For example: Negative things like arguing, throwing stones, gossiping, listening to gossip, being judgmental, making everything about you, are all signs of negative energy and a waste of your time. You will absorb energy people put out be it negative or positive.

Protecting your energy requires knowing when to walk away, hang up the phone or simply saying "I am not having that conversation". Stay away from things that disturbs your peace. When you you're your place of peace, joy surrounds you!

JOY

Day 13

I love the JOY so much, that I came up with an acronym for it:
Just **O**vercome **Y**ou! (JOY)

Once you overcome who you use to be and find peace within yourself, the joy will follow.

It is an amazing feeling to have joy. You learn how to love others experiencing the pleasure that you deserve in life.

God never intended for us to be broken down, sad, or in a negative headspace. Those feelings and emotions are a choice we get to make so, choose Joy!

5 SECONDS

Day 14

Did you realize that it takes five seconds to train your mind to get things done!

Use your five seconds to make the best change in your life and move forward towards your goals and dreams!

Author *Mel Robbins* of the book, *The Five Second Rule*, tells you all you need to know to overcome your 5 seconds.

Try this exercise:

Think about a task you need to complete. Count backwards 5,4,3,2, and before you get to 1 you should already be working towards that task to get it done. Write down how you felt after those 5 seconds?

_____

_____

_____

_____

_____

_____

_____

_____

_____

_____

RECOGNIZE

Day 15

Do you recognize who you really are? Are you focused on how others recognize you?

Write down who you are, to you.

ACKNOWLEDGE

Day 16

Acknowledgement is accepting the truth about yourself and sometimes that is hard for us as human beings to do. We would rather live a lie instead of living our truth. Becoming a better you, requires acknowledging things that you must change.

What is it that you want to acknowledge about yourself, that could help you on your journey to becoming a better you?

_____

_____

_____

_____

_____

_____

_____

_____

_____

_____

_____

_____

ACCEPT

<u>Day 17</u>

Accept the fact that things may not always be the way you prefer them to be. If you keep a positive mindset, and stay motivated toward accomplishing your goals, your reality will become easier to accept and more joyful to experience.

WORTHY

Day 18

You are worthy of everything you pray for and speak into the atmosphere. Appreciate yourself in spite of your imperfections and the physical and emotional scars you may carry as a result of the past.

You are not your past, and you are not your scars.

CELEBRATE

Day 19

Celebrating yourself is an important factor in life. Engaging in enjoyable moments that are important to you is reason enough to celebrate. You do not need anyone to help you feel good about yourself, celebrate regardless of what it is, trust me you will feel amazing.

FAVOR

Day 20

You are a blessing from the higher power He will always shows favor.

Pray for divine favor, it will change your life forever.

What does Favor mean to you on a
spiritual level?

HEALTH

Day 21

You are what you eat!

By no means am I not telling you what to eat but pay attention to what you put into your body,

It plays a major role on how we as people operate.

Food Diary: What are your eating habits now?

WINNING

Day 22

Winning: Is not for the weak! To win, you must do things you have never done before! Take a chance to create your winning reality.

How do you plan to win? What radical action will you take to place you in position to WIN BIG?

_____

_____

_____

_____

_____

_____

_____

_____

_____

_____

_____

_____

_____

YOU CAN!

Day 23

Never say that you can't. ALWAYS TELL YOURSELF THAT YOU CAN!

When you speak negatively, it always seems to find comfort within your spirit. Manifest positivity.

Stay Ambitious!

What is something you've been wanting to do? Write it down then execute it? Believe you can and you will.

_____

_____

_____

_____

_____

_____

_____

_____

_____

_____

_____

_____

BELIEVE

Day 24

Believing in yourself should be your priority.
In order to obtain any goal whether it is a
new career, receiving a degree,
purchasing a home, elevating your faith,
understand that you must believe that you
can accomplish it. Speak it, vision it and
your mind will find ways to do it.

What are some things you want to start manifesting in your life?

Remember believing in you is the key!

_____

_____

_____

_____

_____

_____

_____

_____

_____

_____

_____

_____

_____

MEDIATE

Day 25

Set your timer for 60 seconds. You must be seated for this.

Close your eyes, quiet the noise and just relax.

Sit still for 60 seconds.

Once you reopen your eyes you will feel refreshed.

Try doing this daily to reset and clear your mind if you have a smudge stick use it to create your tone of calmness and peace around you.

How did that exercise make you feel?

_____

_____

_____

_____

_____

_____

_____

_____

_____

_____

_____

_____

_____

PERSONAL

Day 26

Keep reminding yourself that this motivational journey is personal, you owe it to yourself!

What do you wish to accomplish from seeking a deeper personal understanding about yourself?

COMMITMENT

Day 27

Being committed to becoming a better you require discipline. It takes hard work, a ton of dedication and plenty of self-discipline but, you can do it.

EXCELLENCE

Day 28

Be excellent on purpose!

Being excellent is an attitude not a skill and it warrants you to do this on a continuous basis.

PROCESS

Day 29

Once you learn how to process how energy works, how to keep your peace, and the things that motivate you, you will then understand how to apply these things to your daily life, almost effortlessly.

Life is a journey and having positive motivating words behind you can only push you towards peace beyond your understanding.

It will bless you in every aspect of your life beyond measure! Regardless of what life experiences you are facing.

ACCOMPLISHED

Day 30

I leave you with this scripture:

John 19:28 KJV
After this, Jesus knowing that all things were now accomplished that the scripture might be fulfilled, saith, I thirst.

Continue to seek your higher power on your journey. You can look high and low but it will never be anyone greater than your higher power to help you elevate to the next level. I hope my words help you each day, meditate on them daily, as well as your journal reflections. Do this to remind yourself how great you are and how great you can be. Positive thoughts and words are an instrumental part of your journey, to stay motivated.

Write down how accomplished you feel
reading *A Motivational Journey Journal*

REFLECT

Day 31

Reflect back: Which were the most
important days to you?